SAILING TO HOKKAIDO

First published 2001 by
Worple Press
12 Havelock Road
Tonbridge
Kent TN9 1JE

ISBN 0 953947 6 6

Worple Press is an independent publisher specialising in poetry, art and
alternative titles. It is part of The Worple Company Ltd. (Reg. No.
3829499). **Worple Press** can be contacted at:

12 Havelock Road, Tonbridge, Kent TN9 1JE
Email theworpleco@aol.com
Fax: 01732 352 057

Typeset and printed by Peepal Tree Press

JOSEPH WOODS

SAILING TO HOKKAIDO

for Sarah

CONTENTS

What Diogenes was looking for with his lantern was an indifferent man

E.M. Cioran

My heart is in the East
But I am in the farthest West,
How can I taste what I eat,
And how can food to me be sweet?

Judah ha-Levi (c.1075-1141).

SAILING TO HOKKAIDO

After dinner
walk to the stern alone

and look out
for the time it takes

to discern two
darknesses from one.

Suiheesen was the line
where sky and sea met.

For two horizons,
sky and sea

land and sky
there are two words.

Tonight one darkness
overruns another.

There is no line between
the two. Walk back

to the palpable heartbeat
of a generator.

FIRST SHELTER

Taking
shelter from the rain

the
tail-end of a typhoon

among
old men sitting cross-legged.

Listening
to the pelt and words merging

into
a counterpoint I have no ear for.

PERSIMMON

Before
    the tepid jolt
of departure
from Kutsukawa,
the eye catches
a persimmon tree
out of leaf
and persimmons
more orange
for the absence
of leaf.
What is it
with fruit that
takes the frosts
to ripen?

NOT FORGETTING THE WORD FOR WINTER

Mounds of rice-
husks heaped

like sawdust
are burning

in the open
fields.

The chaff
of closure

goes up
in smoke

that tapers
high in this

sky to nothing.
Winter,

and the straw
of others.

WHERE THE WORD FOR BEAUTIFUL IS CLEAN

What brought me out that morning
was the sound of someone on the roof

a monkey glanced down, then stared
away at the something interesting,

eating the core of a stolen apple,
hungry and halfway down its mountain.

I turned to see, snows had arrived
and Kyoto was below in its dip

surrounded by mountains gone white
overnight. For miles between,

millions of roof tiles covered and clean.

NEW YEAR'S DAY, NAGASAKI

Cats have a place in this city,
you can smell them everywhere
and it's good to smell animals
again, even cats.

Or watch them fold into corners
hunting sun in a cemetery
full of offerings; sandalwood
incense, sprays of anise and sake.

At the church of the twenty six
martyrs, you light candles
I wait at the back and watch.

In this light
the light on you,
you move to give
worship a meaning.

I turn to a bay of ships
through a green
and then blue window.

KUNDA BEACH

I sit among the shattered lobster pots
on a tree trunk the ocean has given up.

On the far side of earth where nothing vies
or contests for attention, even the depths

out there seem equally inert. Watching
as a black cormorant bobs on the deep,

disappears and appears again between
parting waves until lost from sight.

The earth is small on a weekday
from a working beach

Sunday of my life.

Come June it will be time again
to reach for the tin on the high shelf,
ignite the green coil and watch
the red tip slowly diminish
the spiral. Undisturbed in the hallway,
a smoke plume rises, mosquitoes
turn languid in its ether,
overcome by Pyrethrum;
essence of that wild chrysanthemum
of the Balkans. Pounded into incense
to burn an acrid smoke. It anoints
each room and feeds the furnace
of summer. A memory, thought
decomposed, composes itself again.

TRIPTYCH

I

From the kitchen of mild odours
a simple meal of rice, beans and miso soup.

Each monk has his own set of eating bowls
which he takes care of, pouring hot water

into each bowl to drink the rinse, so as not to waste
a particle of food. In praise for the minute lives

sacrificed, the time and energy expended.

In the kitchen garlic and onions,
flavours that affect the spirit, are forbidden.

II

Every leaf is heavy here with rain
and a scent of mould rises to muzzle.

Stone lanterns are quenched by the hood of moss . . .

- *Stay long enough and the seasons will create
  the same vacillations they would at home.*

III

Under a monk's calm instruction
I light three sticks of incense,

for God, my ancestors and me.

- *Things are lost because of my English,*
  he says.

Because of *my* Japanese and my English.

EATING OUT

The red-haired Israeli girl
rolled her eyes then flicked
an ash onto a white plate.

Her husband eyed
the stigmata of wine
on the tablecloth

while Julian grinned,
gorged on Chianti
and later retched.

Between arias,
. . . *the Irish can drink*
from ditches for all I care.

A German woman called
to the waiter to silence
Caruso.

That wasn't Enrico,
someone snapped and talk
ebbed to lighter things,

lipstick on nipples or something . . .
I had decided days earlier
to say less.

POSTCARDS FROM THE GATE HOUSE

I

Overnight,
scattered salt
from the smashed
salt cellar
turns to tears
on the linoleum.

II

The damp seals
my unaddressed
envelopes
but can never
send them.

LIGHTHOUSE

Knowing the way
my day's last ascent.

Stub out the cigarette
the glass lung is full

and times' slivers
are shored

my lights are heavy.

CASTING APPLES INTO AN ORCHARD

Noon is a short sigh
before sleep
surrendering to shade
and a memory half-
unleashed,
among wild herbs
and poppies
drying to dust.
Above,
the droning
of an unnamed insect
who shall stay
nameless,
and over there
an orchard I'll never visit

RUMOUR

The untended cemetery in summer
fills with growth.

Headstones bob down in the sea
green of chaos,

each one deciphered in the light
of last February

knowing, what could be got
would never be enough

to know. Everything has a surface
which we undermine

believing in rumours beneath.

KEYS

Wood tablets burning
at the temple,

in clear sunshine the smoke
of spent prayers.

Footfall and crunch
of fine gravel, white

and raked earlier
into a geometry of runnels,

shadows complete the riddle.
A distant key of piano

rehearsal floats by. Here,
among the etceteras

of autumn and place,

I settle up.

IN LAMPANG

The glassless window
wood and light
calando
on your hair
and there
the corner
you nestle in.

Others arrive
will arrive
make purchases
and leave.

Between them,
lunch and the buzzing
of a fly

    too little to gnaw
    or prevent sleep.

A ceiling fan
in your room rotates,
does little
in this heat,
for this heat.

CAO DAI CATHEDRAL, TAY NINH.

The dragons with lion-like heads climbed the pulpit: on the roof
Christ exposed his bleeding heart. Buddha sat, as Buddha always
sits, with his lap empty...

The Quiet American, Graham Greene

At noon prayer
a swallow
above our heads
sideslips
into the jaws
of a clay dragon.

Its forked
tail
an electric flicker,
as it feeds
five hungry heads.

At noon prayers,
the tongue
of a serpent
in the mouth
of a dragon.

LONG WAVE

Turning the dial and though
the batteries are new

the long waves are empty.
From a dead station

the vaguest of sounds,
high-pitched wheezes

delivering the small hours.
They know no ceilings,

straying the boundaries
of a volume on low,

for seconds or even hours
converging

and eloping through my night.

TRANS-SIBERIAN

One evening rolls in
to another,
the sun is a slow
ball sliding
on gunmetal
and nothing much
to do except
take stock,
keep a window
watch and wait
for the next
stop.

In the restaurant
car a samovar
gurgles for green
tea, I gather
the talk
is of movies
while Siberia
rushes by
as one.
So the long
frame of frozen
rivers comes
to close,
I wait for stars
to form
and watch
as ground gives
way to sky.

ISLINGTON

She segments an orange
grills the bacon
and plunges the coffee,
thumbing a local newspaper
sent from home.

The sun is high
through a half-opened window,
blazing on Islington.
Workmen on a roof
pause for tea.

There is a cat
on her window-sill
three storeys up.
I lean out to touch
and its coat toasts my fingertips.

It's already hot outside
and the radio is getting ridiculous.
A resolve of some sort,
even one against me, would do.

SUNNYSIDE

and I have come
from the house
on the precipice,
where the church spires
dip in this heat haze
and the tom

has made a breakfast
of its offspring.

People sit
on the church steps,
engaged in the colours
and languor of day

while milk sours
in a steel jug.

DEAD LETTERS IN DYER STREET

For days we've dug down
through the dryness
for that dark layer of mulch.

By lunch, groundwater seeks
its own level as I'm buried
in the pit to my oxters,

bucketing black to the blue above.
Revealing slime which was surface,
a firmament, where scattered lie

the halves of hazelnuts and oyster shells;
relics of a meal before Kepler walked.
A shard sends out its own light,

in the hand the base of a pinched pot.
Washed, the glaze gleams new
as light redefines it.

My fingers fit perfectly that pinch.
Under the glaze and fixed forever,
lies the fingerprint.

PRIVATE LANGUAGE

for Claudine

Evening and the yellow
bucket lies obvious on the green
of the back garden.

I tell my toddler niece
(rotund in rainbow colours)
to go, get the *yellow* bucket!

She returns, cradling the heads
of early daffodils.

TWO STUDIES OF THE JUMPING CHURCH AT KILDEMOCK

The church didn't jump, only the gable –
forty tons of it leapt inwards.

Declining south, it stands yards away
from its foundations, rising from the bare earth.

A solid mass of masonry, held by the bond
of oxblood, it rests in recoil

from the heretic's grave at the western end.
Like magnets repelled from the same poles,

the heretic held his ground even in sleep,
and the church its shrunken enclosure.

II

So the hand runs over pieces of jamb
and wave-moulded chamfer, to a limestone
lavabo, flower shaped and opening at the centre

where a priest washed hands
under a trickle of water,
poured by an acolyte before the canon.

The rivulets darkening stone petals
to drain through an absent ovary
and out onto the earth.

AFTER THE FLOOD

And the fields from last summer are lakes now,
returning to a place where damp
makes roses on walls inside and out.

The lived-in houses are silent, marked by tide
lines to the windowsill. They sit and wait
under the wash of drizzle and drip.

Bog cotton swells to transparency
and the hooded crow shakes wet from a wing
to shudder straight. Unlike the river,

bent on this season, casting aside the carcass
of a sheep whose legs point to a sky of trough.
An old man, ragged, crosses the demesne,

to a few poles of dead cedar. And turning
he sees me, a withered field between us,
we wave under the same sough.

INTERVIEW

It dances on draughts
that do not disturb me,

a fleck of dust, soaring
the micro-Boreas of a corridor.

I was made wait, and the mind
idles over distance. Somewhere,

a Chaos-butterfly is flapping
its wings. I have no ear

for diminutive beats, and this tremble
is perceptible to the eye only.

Or perhaps a corridor is the bell jar
in that theory. I've attached myself

to dust and feel it in my bones —
if this fleck sinks from sight

it was a bird of ill omen.

AN OCCASIONAL HOUSE OF HER FATHER'S

You loped ahead over fields hardened
by winter, leading me to another secret
place; a cottage consented by your father.
When asked, he simply gave you the keys.

Until now, it had been strange gardens,
private meadows or your favourite table
tombs. And if they weren't secret
they became so, in the hours we visited.

Indoors, you showed me a painting
of a steamship belonging to some ancestor
who had grown up in a dream
of the sea, was swallowed by it.

I could smell apples as my fingers twilled
your hair. You opened your father's room,
bare except for apples. An entire floor
cobbled with windfalls, green as the door
we came through.

The care he had taken with each apple
to mould a practical tapestry for winter.
With a strand of that same care he would
return, winter done, to string himself
to silence and kick away the chair.

TO THE CLIFFS

We walked eight miles to the cliffs,
nobody gave us a lift, we were out
of season. You broke the journey,
imitating the gaits of other patients.
I laughed my head off.

Back in our room, I'm sure they rifled
our bags and found the axe in yours.
All very innocent, holed up in a hotel
that winter. On our last leg,
and they thought we were queer.

THREE TROGLODYTES

Someone slammed the door
on your flight a summer ago.

I had to force it, wood grown
big with the rain, sea-facing,

to almost burst from its frame.
Inside, as if emptiness and dust

colluded in that curve
I was late for the wren,

its neat skeleton stretched against
the pane. Flight-etched and fragile

as the veins of the half-gone leaf.
A pebble head points to green,

unattainable through glass,
grown thin against the elements.

And behind those rib pins,
the nest fluff of a spider. I shuffle

off wet boots and rest myself
beside the range

— content the walking's over
and the door doesn't shut.

BEAULIEU

My sloping valley fills with estuary tide,
up to the halfway lock that dams
the lake, in its turn fed by freshwater.

Moorhen, bald coot and dabchick seek suddenly
the cover of reeds. I've disturbed them
not by sound but unaccustomed colour.

Walking the circuit path where we in conversation
had walked that path, picking our way
and words carefully, spokes in a wheel

that only spun here. Mute and whooper feather
the dark fringes and now, no ruts in the track.
A shelduck loose overhead above trees,

has lost its lustre, in the image catapulting across water.
Among those trees, a Dutch manor
and a legend that Wren had a hand in that plan.

We were wrapped up against the cold,
in ourselves and those deep conversations.
Crossing the stream, I stoop to its shallows

and the life within, a trickle of time taken away.
So the tide deposits salt, not long enough
to sour growth. It recedes, overwhelmed

by overflowing freshwater lake and weir.
At low tide, redshank and dunlin mop
the mud edge of a conversation haven.

DAYS
For Paul Grattan

Days unfurl into days,
the mornings of waking
hopelessly adrift
still exhaling
the air of collapsed
routines.
What keeps me
going is a letter
that needs posting
or the prospect
of one reply.
I shave for ages
and am led
by the dog
to the park
where he runs
wild and I lie
under my tree.
Reaching
for a rationed
Silk Cut
while he noses
at nothing.
My cigarette
smoke lifts
like morning;
it's autumn
and the audible
sticks in combat
are the rut of deer
in the foreground.

Behind the herd
the sun beats
through,
shimmering.
I see an ocean,
wet miles
of transparent
thread, stitching
the green and holding,
holding it all together.

LOSING THE THREAD

It's all fallen apart
your black and ivory silk blouse
the one you loved you let slip
into a bucket of bleach.

Hours lapse in the full
frenzy of house cleaning
as colours leach
to a winding-sheet.

Everything has its run
and what the worm has spun
is now parchment. Retted
useless, it will have to go.

So just drape it
by your window to dry out.
Allow a breeze to arouse
this curtain of your house.

ALL I OWN...

I said I'd take it and move in a week from now,
well received on a second visit
perhaps it was just autumn
and walls taking on yellow.

A step down of course to be back alone in a room
where all I own is all I owe
but there's light, shelves
and a table by the window.

My bachelor uncle lived light years in the space
of a room. They always said
I'd end up like him.

Every family ordains the one who'll be strange,
they do this early on.
My electricity meter
eats 50p's and *Hungry Horace*

is etched above the slot. I'll put coins aside,
and candles where I'll find them.

SICILIAN SKETCHES

...many times I have lost myself in the sea.
Unaware of the water, I go searching a death
in which light consumes me.

Gacela de la Huida, Garcia Lorca

1. Rain

Yesterday's rain of rice on the steps
of the Basilica di San Sebastiano
is rained upon by today's drizzle.

Kernels hold firm against a wind
that will not scatter what the hand has.
Vows are now a day old

and celebrations cease to the clang
of colossal bronze doors,
a sound seal on memory.

Beyond the balustrade, a mere mizzle
has flushed streets clean of activity,
licked the lava pavements and painted

colour on the faces of stone statues.
In the corner of a ricefield in Asia,
a farmer and his wife make love

while seed-shoots are sown
into a waiting earth. I did not see
anything and if I was there,
I was only sleeping.

2. Instructions

Perch yourself on the rocks and prepare
(the good eye on the Ionian)

for the wave to wash over and feed you in.
Take to the swell and aim for the horizon.

Ignore the undertow and slow lung-lapping
then sudden failure to float as a dead man.

Fall into the green, the green arms
of anaesthesia, you are more water now than ever.

3. Flotsam

Hours in a hospital bed where nothing
matters, only the benign
feed of a drip into the left arm.

The indignity of putting people out
and being back again. Whispering
glances at this daft, naked and hirsute

foreigner who took to our waters
and swam out on his own
having no need of Sirens.

My wet lungs for a cigarette,
only hours before the earthly
addictions assail again.

Saved, saved by the grip
of a stranger, the drag ashore
to a voice in the ear that insisted.

How many parts of one drown...
my mother's sister, was she four or five?
A nearly evaporated swallow-hole,

still a Pacific for a four year old:
her father's abandoned herding,
her brown hair, yellow summer dress.

I did not hear anything
and if I was there I was sleeping.

4. Dream

I stand on coarse sand to see
where things meet
my gnarled hands
liquid feet.

5. Villa Palagonia

We pass through a *cordon grotesque*
and into the villa Palagonia,
where each gargoyle
was commissioned by the Count
to drive his wife insane.

Our steps echo on tiles
of an empty ballroom where
mirrors on ceilings once
distorted dancers into monsters.
They have tarnished now to gunmetal

and hardly reflect light. Open shutters
on noon frame a stone demon, leaping
over a wall for two centuries. Three
of us here and the thought of a waltz

dissipates in the heat, fades
like the frescoes of bad taste.
A cat that's strayed inside
stops to lick its paws.

6. Passeggiata

In this immensity my thought is drowned:
And shipwreck sweet for me within this sea.

from *The Infinite*, Leopardi

From the balcony, distant peaks darken
to oriental as evening passes. A square
beneath fills as it has done for centuries,
leaving the countryside to darkness and itself.
The toll of being outside walls still haunts,
only the odd or brave live there.
Now young and old begin the *passeggiata*
circulating through streets into a piazza
and back again; the vascular system
of every southern town. I sip a see-through
wine harvested from the plains below,
my kidneys still sore and sour with salt.
Here, with hardly a notion, I could begin again.
Knowing the heart and some of its arteries.

7. At Cefalu Cathedral

Roger II sailing from Salerno to Reggio in 1131 got caught in a storm and fearing he would drown, vowed to build a cathedral if he survived. He landed at Cefalu.

Churches the world over are
possessed by the same scent

cruets laid on a local lace,
one half-empty, sticky and sanguine.

Christ looks down from the apse,
from gold heights, severe

and Norman as the glint of a blue
eye on this island. His book opened

at the words,
light of the word.

And an Arabic air to this nave, no light
lozenges fall on these flags

— more a glow, while Palermo still looks
east at siesta. The right hand gestures

a Bodhisattva silence, inscrutable
Norman in a mid-day Byzantine gloom.

8. Ice

Perhaps it was an iceberg
That he had glanced at on his journey from Japan.

from *Lough Derg*, Patrick Kavanagh

Brought up to believe
that even walking near water
was enough to draw you in,

the stagnant canal and that pram
rusting among the miasma. Waves too,
in the numerous sea, always away

and never toward any openings.
Then, that journey north where
Japan, ceasing to look like itself,

turned its frontier face
to the frozen sea of Okhotsk.
And on arrival the ice had cracked,

a thaw of yellow slabs creaked
and groaned under the enormous
weight of the break up.

There was nothing to do having
reached it, except stroll on
the grey shore and consider

the journey back. My mother's father,
was seventy odd, when he saw the sea
for the first time and remarked to her

in his soft midlands mantra,
Such a lot of water...
an awful lot of water.

SALVAGING A SWEETNESS

Evening
    and returning
to my room,
      the remains
of breakfast
      on the white
tablecloth
    as we'd left it
in the scatter
      for a train.
The half-drunk
      half-full
cups of coffee
      and thin
slices of bread,
      curled
and baked
    to biscuit
in the all-day
      glare
of absence.
    I crunch
on a piece
    as the sun
goes down,
    my tongue
salvaging
    a sweetness,
a hint of
    honey
and the light
    you leave
in this room.

MRS. MOON

Vibrato of cicada and crackle of a wood fire behind us,
me and the old man sitting on the stoop, chewing betel
to pulp and spitting out its blood. We gaze down
on the darkening valley, peaks rise before us and rice
terraces in their thousands. One hundred and fifty
something on one slope before I stopped counting,

lost in wonder, darkness, and then just losing track
with those walls of stone, drawn a score of centuries ago.
A scaffold or web as if holding the weight of a mountain;
strange how things settle, to take on weight like that.
Like stairs now or steps to the heavens, ascending peaks
that shift, reveal themselves between mists and cloud

of a microclimate. *Here comes Mrs. Moon again ...*
says the old man spitting crimson and turning down
a cigarette *...when Mr. Cloud has gone.* The black
of the highest appears as if disembodied, we thought
we were high and there it is, lost in the negative space
of some vast woodblock print. Moonlight files a glint

over water held in an ancient field. Laughter comes
from the kitchen, old man's wife and you. We've come
through, we've come through. Tomorrow, Christmas Eve,
we'll head down the valley you and I, and there being no paths,
we'll walk the walls, lured by the sound of falling water,
to bathe in the bottomless blue they talk about.

CAGAYAN DE ORO

All night the ship listed and rolled in the swell,
its engines cranking and grinding, keeping us awake,
alert and nervous after upgrading to first class. No
different from tourist class, except for a damp room,
our own portion of deck, but better by a long shot
than economy; leaving you exposed on the lower deck,
the heat of the engines, night, and the air thick
with the crying of children and mosquitoes.

The thought of seven thousand islands and as many
ferries got me through the night, our ship while old
and rusting was once Japanese. Morning then,
and being alive seems more secure in daylight,
we took our instant coffee within sight of land.
A pair of dolphins criss-crossed the prow
and thought better, before departing. Decks filled
and I saw boys diving into the harbour,

surprised they were heading for us, so far out.
Swarming as the ship stalled to point itself right,
darker than the brown they were swimming in.
We looked down from three storeys to their beckoning
as silver flashed in the sun and the scramble for it,
as they dived in the three-second life silver has
from surface to murk. A boy would emerge, placing
one peso in the purse of his mouth.

The brown five-peso coin had no life here, so silver
kept streaming until the throwers grew bored, casting
obliquely to make them work for it, swim the distance
and perhaps miss the plumb fall of the peso. Like throwing
crumbs at carp and watching the mill, it amused, no rope
having gone out yet. A coin aimed accidentally I think, disappeared
near the propeller's churn, then passengers became distracted
with disembarking. Boys struggled ashore with gobs swollen,

one hundred counted for our coffee. One boy rested
on the thick rope that was tying us to Cagayan de Oro.
In local language *cagayan* means shame.
The Spanish struck gold here.